NIGHT OF THE *Luna Moths*

BRONWYN MILLS

Copyright © 2011
Bronwyn Mills
March Street Press
3413 Wilshire
Greensboro NC
marchstreetpress.com
rbixby@earthlink.net
isbn 1-59661-149-9

Luna moth art by
Tracey Saxby,
IAN Image Library
(ian.umces.edu/imagelibrary).

Cover design by
Doug Hagley.

Acknowledgments

Where to start? I wish to thank James Tate and Molly Peacock for their careful reading and generous suggestions along this rather long road; Samuel P. Delany, for his willingness to support my writing; Doug Hagley, for his wonderful cover design; Anya Achtenberg, for numerous incisive discussions; John Ash for those daily calls in Istanbul with poetry on his mind, Eric Darton for so many wonderful and relevant conversations that I can't keep count; Ed Foster, for introducing me to things Turkish; Gene Blanton, for matters piggish; Helen Bartlett, for *her* wit in reading; Helen Cottington, for a harbor in a storm in London; my teachers, Kamau Brathwaite, Ngugi wa Thiong'o, Tim Reiss; Rozan Krause, for unerring positive regard—for me as well as my writing—and all the Epsteins and Dimows, for their love and support; Jennah, Max, Ahli; literary—and literate—friends Moris Farhi; Saliha Paker; Sedat Aybar; Gaspard; Guillermo Cannessa and Vilma, Gonzalo Fernandez; Maria Mora Monje for wood-fired tortillas, *y su padre,* Don Chepe; Geoffrey Sharp; Geoffrey Glick and family; Mestre Joao Grande, for lessons in the value of memory and the poetry of capoeira; Rufin Ahandessi, for the poetry of Fongbe as he taught it to me in Africa; Joseph Adande, for stern poetic advice while in Bénin; Noël Dossou-Yovo, for *his* support there, too; my beloved mother-in-law and friend, Rachel Dimow Epstein, for her consistent love and honest appraisal as she saw it; Diane Sautter Cole, for gentle but firm alleluias, and Ward; Dana Delibovi, for her poetry and friendship over the years; John Bowman, who helped pay the bills with his freelance gigs ("Oh, god, don't tell me I'm supporting a *poet!*"); Cousin Richard and Vivian, Abel, Jonathan; Jonathan Allen, for rides and intellectual stimulus; my student Zuhre, now in London, Tom Laverty, for being a damn good poet; Peter Fisher, for old music, a couch, and Berkeley; Ebubekir Akbalit, rug poetry; Georgina Herrera, *para su poesia Cubana tambien*; Nancy y Marta y Jesús; Bixby, for the wonderful phrase, "literary hairball" when referring to this page; Ray Ventre; Katie, Jaspal; David Robertson, fellow sufferer and discussant; my dear and loyal friend Paula Michtom; and in memory of Ruth and Willy Dimow, who thought it was important.

1

Ant Lion Tango   3
Stories My Mother Never Told Me   4
First Marriage   5
The Season of Splitting Apart   6
Traveling to New Mexico   7
Winter Clothed Him   8
Enemies   9
Twilight   10
Snakes Again   11
Slug   12
Alice   13
Esmeralda   14
Blackout with Pigs   15
Blackout with Pigs II   16
Mamifero   17
Sheep Polka   18
Star-Snouted Mole   19
Last Dynasty   20
Insects   21

2

The Night of the Luna Moths 25
Hospital Visit 26
Le Roi de Coeur 27
What We Carried onto the Staten Island Ferry 28
Fixed Points 29
Cleopatra's Suicide 30
Yo-Yo 31
Bouquet 32
Triolet on the Habits of Southern Owls 33
Blood 34
Moorings 35
The Visit 36
Nativity 37
DMZ 38
Northern *Myotis* Diptych
    Just an Ordinary Bat at Baby Cakes Café 39
    Bat Vespers (High Toned) 40
What They Told Us about the Light 41

3

Autumn   45
The Migrant Hawk   46
White Mother of Tongues   47
Through Your Window   48
Fear of the Dark   49
Menu   50
Houdini's Heart   51
Arboricide on Oak Street   52
Gravity   53
Book of Names   54
The Sphinx and the Evening Primrose   55
Spy   56
The Orange Tree   57
Seeing a Fox in Shutesbury   58

...a poetry stained with soup and shame, a poetry full of wrinkles, dreams, observations, prophecies, declarations of love and hate, idylls and beasts...
—Pablo Neruda, "Some Thoughts on an Impure Poetry"

Dedicated to Noah, Rachel, Isabella, and Will.
Of course.

- 1 -

Ant Lion Tango

Ant, I am the Ant Lion,
stay. I've sifted sand
all day and down the decline
I'll send it, dust your way
let me sip you, lick you, lift you
out of your crust, your carapace
"Take everything, taste, don't waste
a modicum of me, make sod of me,"
you say, "step up, step over my castaway
coil, my crust." Ant, caligulate
thus: think there's no mend to me
that ties can be torn, trust is just
some body born to break into.

Stories My Mother Never Told Me

No myths in my childhood, Mother,
no woman's whisper slipped
through the creviced eye of your
earth; no one unwound a world
with dew drawn from morning's
navel. No shadows passed, blue
as twilight, on the pale walls
of my bedroom. Owl, coyote,
fox or wolf—not my totem.

I had old wives' tales: in the
house a spider means good luck.
Step on a crack, you'll break your
mother's back. Red sky in the
morning, sailors take warning; red
sky at night, sailor's delight.
Dogwood is stunted; from it
came wood from which they hung
Jesus. Coyotes decimate
a flock of sheep; owls snatch
babies; fox's quarry are
innocent chicks and hens;
a wolf will always eat you—

Nature red in tooth and
claw—or not at all.

First Marriage

Then, we woke up peacefully
to sheep chewing grass by the
windowsill—the ram who, love-
struck, nudged me gently, three ewes.
We took nothing but their fleece,

bought a dog—Branislav, a
St. Bernard, named for a man
in an old Polish movie—
fenced the sheep with woven wire
hand-stretched, gate tied shut with rope.

Branislav would bark at them
one-hundred and eighty pounds
of dog dancing side to side.
Just play. But when I left you—
stumbled, ignorant of love, of

loss, I heard Branislav bit
the head off one, then stood in
our driveway, bloody with
a hard-on, incapable
of understanding what he'd
done.

The Season of Splitting Apart

> (...in the Chinese book of wisdom, the *I Ching*,
> what follows the hexagram K'un when the top line
> moves. Of that line it is said: "Dragons fight in the
> meadow/ their blood is black and yellow.")

April's full yang moon began with an eclipse—
Then there were three days of hollow nights,
the nights when we woke to the flat moon
staring us in the face, scattering the shadows
around our bed with its gaze. In the next light,
the sun slipped past its meridian, bringing
the first warm days to New England.

I got up at four-thirty in the morning,
drove the truck down our lane
with the full moon at home's end. Evergreens
broke the pink edge of the horizon in front.
I entered the clearing:

Imagine a single note plucked from a
Chinese lute. Imagine that last summer's cattle
reappeared. They stood in that sound, silent,
each stretching their great bracts toward the moon
like the blanched wingspan of a pterodactyl. Through
the channel of evergreen and birch, the purple hills
heaved their saurian backs against the rising sun.

The sun. The moon. The rising sun, the setting moon—
each in its fullness, they teetered on the rim of the earth
as if it were no more than a pie plate. Dragons like
alley cats, facing off and marking their turf.

This is called "Splitting Apart": when
the battle ensues.

Traveling to New Mexico

for miles a palm extended, this
dry hand holds an ancient sea of life
forms that are fossils now & pulls
the heat from diatomes beneath.
listen, listen to the last ticking
of Pleistocene bones, to the old seabed
that rippled rises to finger mound
traces the weight of dinosaurs
foraging in swampland gone to seed.

in West Texas oilfields steel brontosaurae
stitch beginnings and endings to heat
and dust. Here, we are strangers
skimming the surface, imagining lives
of animals millions of years ago—
30-foot sharks with teeth like fists
distances shrunk by reptilian cries
against advancing thirst.

we bottom-feeders ride lost currents
on the plains, the easing desert—
never leaving boundaries behind

"Winter clothed him...
The furriers Night and Winter."
      —OSIP MANDELSTAM

    November night: cats next to
    the fire, stretched on the rock
    hearth where the stove chirps, stuffed
    with birch, red oak, dead sugar
    maple. Karamazov
    (Fyodor) dozes on the slate
    the double-pawed one called
    Raskolnikov coughs behind
    the firebox, orange fur hot
    when you lift him off the stones.

Enemies

It moved me that the cat hurt his paw,
limped in, growling, then balked
at your touch and ran under a chair. I held
his flanks, pulled, discovered a blood-caked welt
on his foot, parted his fur to find what cause it
    and saw

more dried blood, toes mauled
so they printed red when he set his paw down—
maybe he'd met a 'coon, forgot the stealth
that moves us

when an enemy is near, the lesson of the close call;
but the foot swelled up, got lamer. By nightfall
he let us put him in a box with a towel
and carry him to the vet's; though his pelt
shuddered under your hands, he left them unclawed.
That moved us.

Twilight

The owners, two old people, bolt the door to the bungalow,
and the horse dozes, so dark against the mahogany trees
all you can see is feet
as, far in the corner, the bell-shaped white, white geese
toll their watches— "all's well, go to sleep."

Along the road, two new houses stand, steel doors
painted over and gleaming like teeth.
This was the wild land with an eye
to the drips and trickles that grow into streams.
This was the roadside with old oaks and hemlocks
with needles padding the paths underneath.

Now there are two old people in a bungalow
who tend a garden, an old horse and some geese.
They have parted the land from its bones,
selling it like ancient Pharisees,
piece by piece and even leaf by leaf.

Snakes Again

that slither into my morning dreams
—they do this in huge, hideous coils;
I wake up in a sweat, stifling my screams.

I search my psyche for the usual themes:
my pact with some evil and the spoils
I get for my sin—the glitter that gleams

the scot-free pleasure with no visible seams
but for those unsubtle serpents who foil
my sleep—wake me sweaty, stifling my screams.

I'm in a subway; two men, in front of my seat
each with a snake, cuddling their neck, loyal
to no one, splitting their tongues in my dream.

the largest uncoils, sinks a fang into one of my feet
its man leans down, bites the back of its neck. It recoils.
I wake in a sweat, mouth full of screams.

Slug

Unshelled, it does not creep along
the greaseless weep of gravel
but glides, this beast so like lungs,
whose whole breadth breathes, its trail

so slow we've named someone dull
for it. Slug. Feeds on complex
molecules of just plain air
lays down its own path, simplest

for its elegance, the smooth
way its antennae glance
at the weather, look for damp
secrets and find entrances

that slide, mute, into the heart
of matter and that lay low
to the ground, remembering
the coiled shell, its embryo.

Alice

We did not know Alice was so far gone
when we came to bury her. She'd fallen in the field,
her tummy swelled, feet up, the grass a shield
against the real view of how she'd gone.
An old sheep, she'd been mother to our four
ewes and one ram—maybe she'd eaten nightshade
or poke? So our friend, Peter, my ex-, and I dug
a hole, made bad Hamlet jokes, then lugged

the corpse to the edge of its grave and shoved
Alice into the ground. Peering from above
we saw her bloated stomach had opened up: all
inside was a wavering wall of maggots, crawling:
of course, she'd been done for, for several days.
Death is gauche, we thought, as the sun lifted the haze.

Esmeralda

What a hog. She was black and bulbous,
a bristled sow. Six hundred pounds
past market weight.
Every time the truck made it to the turnaround
she'd greet us there, a stately delegate
of total noir. enormous.

We'd escaped the trucks on First Avenue, metallic
and indifferent, the lean and uncooked
burglar crackhead bum…
Esmeralda loved our touch, tummy
rub or a scratch behind the ears
no species rut, or something phallic

to disturb her post-piglet years. We'd come
to be soothed by the quiet country life
Harry would feed us,
rent us a house; we'd sow vegetable seed, grow
looseleaf, Big Boys, Silver Queen—"have a side
of pork," he said. Tender just for us.

Blackout with Pigs
(Jersey City, August 14, 2003)

In Ed's kitchen, no A.C.,
hot, humid, Gene filling plastic
balls with peanuts for the pigs'
"exercise." Barefoot, I sip
Turkish rakı after Ed's
special dish—"the Imam fainted,"
(it was *that good*.) Afterwards
pig flop, *Porcus porcae*, Pig
of Pigs! Egypt's Great Pig Set—
Oh, to scratch the silk behind
the palm of those ears again;
candlelight, Tibo's soft neck on
one bare foot; Lonnie's, on
the other.

Blackout with Pigs II
(for Rachel)

Well, here's the story of the real pigs:
I made a campaign, getting pictures of them
hung on the fridge: one, a farmer
holding a hoglet, beaming, as if it were
a love affair between 'em. Might as well have
been a handful of pork chops
or some other bloody bauble—
after all, what were we doing except
raising them to be eaten?
We'd toke up, send the pigs out to pasture
and watch. Rudy the Red, the enthused porker
who would climb into the trough, lie there
with a crinkled mouth—piggish grin, sopping
up morning mush through his skin;
the spotted hog who'd run circles around the
pasture perimeter, the fastidious, the devil-may-care-ish
each pig was its own personality. But we eat them!
I want you to know—pigs are seldom what they seem
mothers rowed with tits—ah mother goddess!
one dear piggy masquerades as cream—the
other as a blackout.

Mamífero

A warmer word, Spanish for
"mammal," with "mamí" within
implying, of course, tits
that which distinguishes us
from the feathered and finned;
sino—that is to say, "but"—
for *monotremata,* the
platypus, with poison spurs
that getcha when it's gotta;
when gonadal, it's grumpy
No platitude, says Nash, its
electro-sensitive bill,
duck nose, rhynchal radar reads—
not scents—but sputters, currents
from small, potential prey;
oviporous platys leak
milk, platypussies lap it,
love it, leave it at five months.

Sheep Polka

It's not because I dance with liquor that I do—
I'd wear my boots regulation Montana length
but I'm eccentric, I like the sheep, I do.

By law we wear our boots a certain length
because it's known of men, these parts, they like
the sheep too much; loneliness corrupts our sense,

if not booze. According to some poet we make monsters
in this way, then store them in a jar. What's
the real story? It's us. We're the monsters,

though I don't know how: nothing has touched
you in a long, long time; an innocent animal goes bleating
right by. Your parts move like something rusted

underneath a pile of leaves. The unspeakable bleating
continues and the anger inside—empty, unrequited
—drives you home in only one direction. Screaming,

not bleating, she lunges free after you are done,
and you don't ask, whatcha doing on the plains alone?
it doesn't matter. Could be a ewe, a woman, either one

and its not because I dance with liquor that I do—
I wear my boots past the set Montana length
I'm eccentric, I prefer the sheep, I do.

Condylura cristata
(The Star-Snouted Mole)

Knobbed tail, that's what it means,
but that's a mistake. The detail's
in the nose—imagine! life
with *that* stuck on your face,

each birthstar sealed in parchment
like a caul. Its cold fire blooms,
you are flower faced; your feet
row through the earth, rotifer
nosed, trembling and tentacled;
moleskin suit, waterproof—
twinkle twinkle little snoot,
something's alive below you.
You plow through deep snows, feel
beneath frosted ground—worm's fright;

mole's delight.

Last Dynasty

That winter, the Emperor went mad
left his spouse and heirs a palace in New Jersey,
an estate in the Berkshires, a summer place in Connecticut
and enormous debts from gambling.
The Empress was not prepared.

Years later, she would say, "green wood
gives no heat," leaving the interpretation
up to you. Then, it was just struggle.
She turned the palace into a boarding house,
The Emperor wandered on the grounds and only came
to pound at his piano—even the Empress's shouts
failed to drown him out. The boarders were beside
themselves: their hostess could not cook,
His Eminence was nuts, their blue-blooded babies
were always crying, as the Empress could not nurse.
"Your milk is turning green," her physician said.
"That, too?" she cried & lined up each child
on a pillow, a glass bottle at its side.

The estate went bankrupt. And when
two former courtiers bought the place,
they split it like a melon, each giving
each a lovely view—the Empress and her
entourage caught a commuter car off
to Connecticut, to mourn and reminisce.

The children scattered. One married
an engineer; another went to sea. The last
stayed with them, sworn to her parents' fealty.
The Emperor remained insane. The Empress
entertained: she told stories of when she'd been
Belle of Georgia, and then the Emperor came.

Insects

Rain is incessant this spring,
mudpuddles eternal. Gnats
erratic throng over spring
ponds where mosquitoes like cats
keen while they are breeding;
every two weeks they crack
their membranous eggs, leaving
their watery runways of black
acid rain. In formation,
C5As (which are huge, matte
colored, army green planes in

the shape of great bees) pack
up their guns and start flying
en route to one more Latin
conflict. This is the fast
lane, blood time. They fatten the
season, pests in past perfect.

- 2 -

The Night of The Luna Moths

We had a full moon, mist
and hundreds of luna moths—like hankies
flitting down, or hinged florescent palms
an eye under each thumb. Two of us driving
to Shenandoah; moths crowded
in beam of light that pointed to the side.
"What is it, Ed?" First to find
a motorcycle wreck. Just one young guy,
you know how messy these are—
Ed tried to make sure I didn't see
but it was a long night, moon pacing the asphalt,
no phone anywhere. VW bus drove up,
valves out of time. A semi-, a ¾-ton truck;
gas smell, some kind of electrical fire;
and we were stuck in the middle of a traffic
jam. A trucker called in the cops
on his two-way radio. Then the frogs
started coming out, first one
then another, like the road
was a river and some small boy
was skipping pebbles across the shallows,
another, another, then another. Ed
got right in the thick of it, all six-foot-three
of him breaking the light, bent over that poor kid.
Came back to open the trunk, not a word,
frisked the trash. Went back.
Got into a discussion with the crowd—
Red flashers throb, no more moths, little frogs
back flipped out of the way, not soon
enough for the ambulance to take
off. Back at the wheel
shaking his head; "I gave him
a blanket; but he got scared," Ed
sighed, driving right through
the absence of light.

Hospital Visit

"Can you fix my garter belt?"
that old scow, my mother, is sinking from wear
"—Can you cut it with a pair of scissors?"
"It's a bandage, not a garter belt," I yell,
"You've been hurt." How her chest
is slowed on this sea, steadied by a hospital bed
bound by foam restraints, bandage tape,
an IV drip drilled into her damaged arms
a broken hip holding new false hope—
"You don't understand," she sighs, "do you?"
Wrenching her restraints, wrists flutter,
settle on the rails of her bed.
I hold her small, stiff hand, "It's got
two little things, they attach with teeth—"

Le Roi De Coeur

The movie's now a classic. Alan Bates,
mild and British, escapes the terrors
of the First World War. at the gates
of a French madhouse, he chooses to err
with lunatics, all dressed up and dancing,
not with men in their shirtsleeves killing.
He tries to show them out. Once. At the advancing
sounds of war, men moaning, explosions filling
the screen with guttural roars, they shook
their heads. No way to survive out there.
Like the times you and I look at leaving,
the terrors of going it alone—Let's pretend,
mon coeur—dance with me! It's nineteen-seventeen.
we are Romanovs. King and queen.

What We Carried onto the Staten Island Ferry

she comes in a box   caught in brown paper and cord
we unwrap and untie   take off the top
ground up grey powder   graveled white
that white is   wheels with lace sides
obdurate mass   modest but made to last
she drove   dangerously
on the opposite side   she slid
didn't know what happened   who hit who
but she skidded   then slept several years
died dozens of times   they denied
thwarted by steel   machines that ticked
the bones   kept their burden
forced flesh   food dropped through a tube
stopped   so she died
   We scatter your first woman   your wife.

Fixed Points

The pole star never thinks suicide
—only our tiny sun even
considers dying.

Cleopatra's Suicide

Imagine putting an asp
to your breast, your nipple passed
on to a poisonous snake,
a reptile who takes a fast
bite, unable to resist
the warmth of your blood as it slips
through your vessels like ice floes
broken, crowding the sluices to tip-
toe through early spring, creaking
like ships, like Anthony leaving
—the hypocrite! how he warmed
to heated blood, armed weeping.

Yo-Yo

It's a skill I never learned,
how to fall with grace, then bound
up again, as though I turned

gyroscopically, having found
an eternal gravity within free-fall
How do I rise and tumble with grace, then bound

in diastole, no force at all,
holding on to ordinary string?
With perpetual gravity and free-fall

I should curl up like a tiny spherical thing
unmindful of you and so unfurl along
the comforting twine, descending a string

which doesn't pull near as strong
as your Aztec sacrifice of living parts
that grasp at you; you cast flesh along

the strange path you've taken to heart's
ease. It's a skill I never learned
how to make a sacrifice of livid parts,
rise and fall on similar terms.

Bouquet

Tulips lean
over the kitchen table
telling lies about winter

You tell lies
smooth as petals
in this forest of blood

out in the igneous snow
you look up, "Look at those stars.
they will warm you."

But stars are years away from warming.

Antediluvian fires,
ash by now,
    I lie about their comfort

remembering your eyes
blue starlight
striking you in the face

your flowers
    dying on the table.

Triolet on the Habits of Southern Owls

Down South the owls mate at the end
of August. when the fireflies have run
out of light and cows' udders distend

Owls sigh in the sycamore trees and lend
each pinion and breast to the air, then
moan like cows when their udders distend
and someone must milk them. First one,
then another feathered heart unbends.

Blood

Red efts cross my dirt lane
they're young newts in progress
they're crimson lizards, feigned

landmovers, they are less
amphibious than flame;
their spots signal distress

eight sparks spell their names
on livid bloodless backs;
you toss them in the flames

legend says (this torture lacks
conviction) they are unscathed,
neither consumed nor back

to the same red. Old and unbathed
their time in water lasts
long enough to be betrayed

by the fact of birth. Nothing lasts,
you know that. From its egg
to its eft, to its past.

Moorings

This season, I listen for the geese
to press a creaking prow
through my sleep, to move my dreams
to water I can hardly reach
these days. They do this every year

leave, return, mark the time without device.
They counter thunder going South. They
scatter in the sudden rain
like leaves that blacken pavements when
they rot. Yearly they are different

but the same. They vanish in the air.
For all I know they turn to dust or ash,
but come again. And this is their constancy.
So I listen—since childhood I listen at night

preferring not to see the geese
wanting just their foghorn's call—
"sleep tight! sleep tight!"

The Visit

I go home to this: a flatness stretches
beside the tracks, the shudder my train makes
as it sloughs past brackish Delaware marshes,
the heron crowded into smaller and smaller spaces

as tides give way to dreary business places,
to EXXON, MOBIL, landfill, hedged investments
hopes of gain, no losses. Weeks, I've waked
with the thought of going home, a flatness stretches

back to my childhood, what survival outguesses,
the way to read a room before you enter, the wait
for nothing, the stares at my father's death, his loss
right on the tracks, the shudder the train makes

when it hits child and man stalled in a Chevrolet,
Mother's indifference to that, my ride that expresses
nothing—a way back, a duty I make
—as we slough past brackish Delaware marshes.

Too short of memory to see the vestiges
of him in me, their daughter, my mother delays
and delays her dying. Forty years she's wasted.
Like heron crowded into smaller and smaller spaces

our bonds get lost, they are defeated in stages
the broken surfaces of water, armed whispers,
embraces denied or vicious—who's this strange
woman all bent over; who visits?

I go home to this.

Nativity

Slowly laboring up to the sixth floor
(seven flights counting the front stoop,
she counts the days before
the birth; step by step her sloped
belly ripples under her breast as the baby
treds water, counting the time, always
naming the hours she calls them "Maybe"
or "When," and so its feet feel for the days
of passage. Curbside,
                    trash collectors
drive wide-hipped steeds. Their teeth chew
barrels full of meat wrappers and garbage. Something mews
in the clank and churn of this week's selected
silage, and when the gears stop, the men are wild
—not a kitten, as they counted, but a newborn child.

DMZ

This eclipse of ours, this cliff
rises, devised to defeat us
more a gully, moor or gulf
not the rock, not the rocky
dolmen but a fastness, lengthened
erasures. spaces. its silent
chasms made with raised arms, ruined

landscapes hand carved by combat.

Northern *Myotis* Diptych

1. Just an Ordinary Bat at Baby Cakes Café

My my, *myotis!* You old Moth-eater!
I say, seeing him hanging
over a cup of coffee
at the counter. How's the
missus? His voice is distant,
faint. *We waitin'*, he finally
answers. They fornicate, you
see, hibernate in winter till,
not to be too clinical,
spring; supposedly the sperm
then gets chummy with the egg,
mitosis, or is it mi-
osis?, is set into motion—
reremowse multiplyeth!
Funny weather this season,
we nod in agreement, *Well,*
my leather-wingéd friend lifts
his warm translucents—long those
thin webbed fingers!—*Gotta go.*
Off he loops, head down, swoops,
nips a gnat that got too close.

2. Bat Vespers (High Toned)

This *myotis* is a moth-eater—long eared, its
sonar tunes to flutter, doom
and feathered rust. Sphinx
at its evening primrose,
unfurls its tongue to sink
into that gold chambered bloom
that afterglow—does it know
vesperilionidae
—that is, the bat who flies
lifts warm-whispered wings
carries off moth, crane fly,
midge, more small gnatish things?
The Bat breeds, waits till spring
then embryo cells resume
their Great Divide. Pups arrive
but once per year, when the
flitter-mouse mama, furred, sings
her suprasonic lullaby...

What They Told Us About the Light

It shows life in an egg,
connects light and dark in a winter hearth
fuels the heat of touch, marks the zone of safety
in urban fastnesses, holds prison guards
behind barbed wire

They told us,
they told us that the light
was god come home to read, was
the nightlights of succeeding generations.
They did not tell us it was power
They did not tell us of the fabrication
of bombs, made in this manner:

>	Peel skin, part fat
>	to muscle to bone, slice to marrow,
>	remove single cells. Probe molecule, atom,
>	nucleus, proton, photon, electron, to the least
>	divisible, unseen by mirrors
>	or artificial light.
>
>	See shadows.
>	Wanting power, split the light,
>	in one greedy moment strike the marrow
>	of the marrow of our bones

with dreadful teeth.

- 3 -

Autumn

You want to lift the curtain
of clouds from the sky
or plunge deep in a leaf
before it disintegrates. You want
to crack the jacket of frost
around the meadowgrass
and catch the sap descending
before the sense of loss
weighs down your dreams, bending them
as thunder bends the trees.

The Migrant Hawk
(for Noah)

That eye hidden in the beam
swoops down like a red-tailed hawk
the eye that follows me
each year, down the half-mile walk
toward necessity—

That eye comes home on the western light
unblinking, it breaks and enters the panes
the eye that bars the night gains
each year, imprisoned by sight,
driven down the half-mile of my lane
toward the necessity
of its leaving.

White Mother of Tongues

First, it was only the river
overflowing, a swollen tongue
that sought its proper courses.

Then, it was the omniverous mouth
of infancy feeding on each
sound. We suckled vowel
and consonant, glottal stop
and sibilant. We listened
at our mother's throat.

She cooed like a mourning
dove under the hedges;
she smiled like the crescent
moon, imprisoning us
forging her imprimature
upon what drives
our tongues.
She grasped our heartbeat
in her teeth.

Thus prepared, she showed
us how the world was
meant to be—she had already
lied on how it was.

Through Your Window

Three wild ducks
flutter
beyond pine boughs, trembling
like butterflies
in the sunlight.

They skim
the lake and
hide
in the rising mist,
break
the flat surface
with wings tipped.

From the bed
we share
& through your window
we breathe
cold spring
three wild ducks
sift through
the air.

Fear of the Dark

I write to keep the silence back
beyond my barbed fence of light.
It inches forward instead & I catch
a fleeing heel. It sheds its stare,
that old subterfuge hovering over me,
till my pencil stops rubbing the page
and it pounds away in the noiseless night.

I pursue. It edges down the stairs
leaving a tuft of itself on a carpet tack.
I think I hear a rustling in the well,
it turns: it has a savage, animal face.
Now, alone, I shudder going down
and I pace each step, moving very slow,
and I know, beyond a doubt,
There is where it waits.

Menu

An old woman in a rowboat crouches at the end of a line and rod. She lives in a cabin by the village reservoir. Half a greenhouse snuggles up to one side of the cabin; on the other, a plaster Virgin waves at passersby. Last week, the old woman's grown kids packed their pick-ups and drove home, carried off the "Do Sports, Not Drugs" bumper stickers, the cases of Miller's, and the grandson hiding, skinny and shivering in the truckbed, the older sister counting, "One hundred and one, one hundred and two…"

She fixes the bait on her hook. The moon is rising from the water's rim Somewhere in the middle another moon is floating like a hatchet fish, sleepwalking toward another hook.

Houdini's Heart

> "Some afflictions borne by the brain
> would blow up the heart (like a mine)"
> —Jorge Luis Borges

The body is a diamond, faceted
turned weightless on weight-bearing parts
its bones whisper and its marrow rustles,
it shifts on feet like forests, root crystals shot
into crevice, underground rock

Heat measures the distance,
body to body, of eye from glance
flesh from skin. Then

in the gray stew of the brain
we parse our thought, mold its clay
hold the plastique where love's terrors lie.
The skull is a geode, a mirage. There
memory quivers, arms rush out
in camouflage—
the heart is a garnet

twinkling in the body's cave
pounding like a stranger's footsteps
shackled by veins & arteries
but brave, oh so brave.

Arboricide on Oak Street

Summer stutter on the street—chain
saws strike the trunks of maple trees,
capable muscle and stubborn bone,
stiff, bite into the meat of centuries.
Not an oak to be seen, just sugar maples
one on the corner, marked with a large red "X"
and so big, must be *two* centuries,
and the grey-haired graphic artist, living
in a brick cottage beside it fights for
its life with the city's hard-hatted crew.
At dusk that afternoon, I lean my bike
against the side of the house, look
down the gallery of green yard and see
a mother and her young pup. Two streaks
floating across the lawn. Swimming
through the air and barely touching
the ground, they slip over a dead stump,
ears folded close to the head, the little
one bouncing up and down. How many times
I leaf through *Michigan Mammals*—a mink?
way too small for what I saw. A fisher?
its neck is too thick; an otter's fluid crawl? yes,
but what the heck would they be doing
this far from the lake? The artist staked
his claim and won; the sugar maple remains;
I'd like to think that sylph and its child
escaped the neighbor's dogs, yapping
after their musk, northern river otters
on the lam, like us, doing what they must.

Gravity

> And he was afraid and said, How dreadful
> is this place! this is none other but the house of God,
> and this is the gate of heaven.
> —GENESIS 29:17

In a dream, Jacob set his ladder
against the marquee: angels scatter
overhead, they leap up like salmon,
sides gleaming; their descent was sadder
than the sun going down, fluorescent for
the miracle matinee, blessing
the salmon and the fishermen's net
meant to catch them. Jacob will beget
holy families with mortal seed,
stringing his sperm like fish eggs, fat beads

on stone pillows for angels who leap
at God's promises. What do they see
when the price of promises, like beads,
is a sleek fish filled with reasons?
Jacob's adversaries rise and fall
against holy gravity, a squall
of flurried light that will not leave him
alone one minute, waking or sleeping:
as common as dust, the Divine face
stares back at him from every place.

Book of Names

"The disease develops, and the patient begins to lose
the self," the doctor says. Alzheimer's. True,
I thought, hearing the diagnosis, but that presumes

she's got something to lose. Not my mother. She paid her dues
by doing and expending nothing; no self took root
in that slow-circling mind of hers that would always lose

track of names and relations, even Before. Like whose
daughter I was (out cold when I was born, the memory she'd choose
was the sight of a cemetery outside her window. She presumed

my birth was a wound, a disease.) Diagnosis: "neglect and abuse—
suspected." A lack of interest, insufficient food,
confusion—sometimes I was her mother, then she'd lose

track, think I was her sister, Elizabeth, or I'd fuse
with the image she had of my father—dead, who'd never choose
this for me; but when I fought back, she'd use

all the names in the book: "when your child asks for bread who
among you will give...a stone?" that's what it says in her Book.
But what if you think you've no bread or stones to choose?
What's the diagnosis that presumes?

The Sphinx and the Evening Primrose

For hours we sit in the laps of our lawn chairs,
watching the evening primrose at dusk.
It's gray buds tighten first as light airs
its linen. Still no golden eye unhusks
to find out daytime secrets. Then the click
of its calyx calls the sphinx moth to straddle
its yellow hips, to part the creased pod and slip
inside the flower's sunny lips—it unravels
at this mothy lover's touch. The primrose
unfolds its skirt of lemon silk. It glows.

For hours we sat in the laps of our lawn chairs:
primrose after primrose opened in the night air;
at each, an inscrutable sphinx moth whirred,
warmed each burnished blossom and purred.

Spy

She'd locked the door again, and through the panes'
reflection, afternoon sun near setting,
I saw her watch the yellow bus turn in the lane
and open. I walked its length, my arms getting

unhinged by the weight of lunchpail and books. Yet, in
sight, she didn't seem to hear my knock. Way
in back of the room, too busy forgetting
she'd locked the door again, and through the panes'

reflection, she addressed No One, explaining
the house routines, how to do them, setting
the plates on the dining room table …she didn't pay
attention, this afternoon, to the sun threading

beams through hanging plants, or just setting
"Let me in!" She might've seen but stayed
pretended not to hear the driver near jettison
the gears, backing the bus out of the lane.

The edge of the sky grew redder, fire frayed
and scattered scales and feathers, ball plummeted.
Still warm from walking, my blood remained
persistent. But knocking was hopeless. Letting

my school things go, I made a fist, hitting
the pane, "Let me in!" the sound of glass breaking,
and my mother let me in; she was sweating.
Blood was on my hands. "You broke the glass!"

        She locked the door again.

The Orange Tree

One sweet memory squeezed
from the woman who hated them both
like an animal who'd been tethered
yet failed in every escape. He didn't know,
simply put it all aside—charcoal, clay,
copper plate. later it was Biblical,
"I washed her mouth out with soap." Even the eggs
would be ready to explode, and when she
—or he—got furious, there were oranges
to cut, to turn on a blunt glass point,
fruit spurting topaz seed,
slippery with milt. Setting each of them
a glass, she said: "Don't swallow those pits.
A tree'll grow right out of your mouth."

I could see it: big, glossy, two-hearted leaves
cracking my breath with its citrus smell
words green and thorny with hope.

Seeing a Fox in Shutesbury

Behind a larch this morning
Eurydice turns into a fox. Through
bare landscapes of scrub and granite
she floats onto the meadow
fifteen yards below the garage.

Lightly, this somnambulist
wraps herself in red, ear tips dark,
and with forward-moving innocence
steps precisely. Feline.

She knows her place in the world
which others have forgot.